# THE ALGONQUIANS

# PATRICIA RYON QUIRI

# THE ALGONQUIANS

*Franklin Watts*    *New York*    *London*    *Toronto*    *Sydney*    *A First Book*

# *Acknowledgments*

Special thanks to Sylvia Kelly and Bob Lynch of the BOCES Geneseo Migrant Center in Geneseo, New York, for their generosity and help in researching information for this book

1266 2744

Map by Joe LeMonnier
Cover photograph copyright © Smithsonian Institute, Photographic Services (#81-6780)
Photographs copyright ©: Nawrocki Stock Photo, Chicago: pp. 3, 12 top, 23, 29, 32, 39, 45, 50;
National Gallery of Canada, Ottawa, Gift of Robert Lindsay Estate, 1990: p. 10; The Royal Ontario Museum, Toronto, Canada: p. 12 bottom (painting by Paul Kane); North Wind Picture Archives: pp. 17, 28, 37, 43, 48; National Geographic Society: p. 19 (painting by Langdon Kihn); Smithsonian Institute, Photographic Services: pp. 21 (80-19876), 35 (87-6569), 38 (80-16639), 41 (77-5613); National Museum of American Art, Washington, DC/ Art Resource, N.Y.: p. 24; Buffalo Bill Historical Center, Cody, WY: p. 26; Library of Congress: p. 31; American Museum of Natural History: p. 33 (#1487-2, photo by Rota); Indian and Northern Affairs, Canada: pp. 53, 54.

Library of Congress Cataloging-in-Publication Data

Quiri, Patricia Ryon.
The Algonquians / by Patricia Ryon Quiri.
p.  cm.—(A First book)
Includes bibliographical references and index.
Summary: Describes this noted Indian civilization, including its arts, crafts, religion, and daily, social, and political life.
ISBN 0-531-20065-5
1. Algonquian Indians—Juvenile literature.  [1. Algonquian Indians.  2. Indians of North America.]  I. Title.  II. Series.
E99.A35Q58   1992

970.004′973—dc20

91-29111 CIP AC

# CONTENTS

*For my mother-in-law, Betty Quiri,*
*one of my best friends*

# INTRODUCTION

Long before the Europeans came to the shores of the New World, other groups of people lived throughout the continents known as North and South America. These people became known as "Indians."

Scientists believe the ancestors of the Indians did not originate in the Americas. *Archeologists* have found no proof of pre-Stone Age humans on either continent. Thus scientists have accepted the theory that the ancestors of the Indians were originally from Asia.

Scientists believe that between fifteen and forty thousand years ago, some inhabitants of Asia might have wandered to North America in search of food, probably by way of the Bering Strait. This body of water between the Soviet Union and Alaska is about 56 miles (90 km) long. Scientists think the Bering Strait might once have been land. If it was, the ancestors of the Indians could have walked from Asia to North America. If not, they may have migrated by canoe.

THE OIL PAINTING, *INDIANS IN A SNOWY LANDSCAPE*,
BY C. KRIEGHOFF, SHOWS MUCH ABOUT ALGONQUIAN LIFE.
NOTE THE CRADLEBOARD, MOCCASINS, AND
SNOWSHOES THE INDIANS ARE CARRYING.

Tens of thousands of years ago, these people were wanderers. Their only concern was survival. They followed and hunted large animals, including bison and the woolly mammoth. Perhaps these great animals led them to the Bering Strait and into North America.

Scientists think it took thousands of years for those groups of Asian people to migrate into the Americas. They probably roamed in small groups. As the years passed, different groups pushed southward and eastward. They settled in the northwest, southwest, around the plains, throughout the Great Lakes and into Canada, down into Central and South America, and into the eastern portion of North America.

Why were the ancestors of these Asian people called Indians? They were so named by Christopher Columbus in the 1490s. He had set sail across the Atlantic Ocean from Spain in search of a new route to the East Indies. When his ships reached land, he thought he had indeed found the East Indies. Therefore, he called the people living there "Indians." It was not realized until later that Columbus had, in fact, discovered a new world previously unknown to the Europeans, a vast stretch of land later called North America. Thus, the people he encountered were wrongly named. However, the name "Indian" has stuck with these people. Descendants of the Indians are often called "native Americans." This is a

TOP: COLUMBUS'S ARRIVAL IN NORTH AMERICA
HERALDED A NEW ERA FOR BOTH THE
NATIVE INHABITANTS OF THE CONTINENT
AND THE EUROPEANS. BOTTOM: TRIBE MEMBERS
READY A MEAL OVER A FIRE.

more appropriate title, as the word *native* means "belonging to a place by birth."

This book will focus on a group of Indians collectively known as the Algonquians (sometimes spelled Algonkians). They were so named by the Europeans who settled in North America. The white settlers met a tribe called the Algonquins (note similar spelling) who lived near present-day Quebec, Canada. The Algonquin language was similar to that of other Indian groups in the northeast. Therefore, the Europeans applied the name Algonquian to many Indian tribes.

The Algonquians settled in the northeast woodland sections of North America. There were many tribes within the Algonquian-speaking Indian family who lived in the Atlantic woodlands and around the Great Lakes. There were also Algonquian tribes who lived along the eastern side of the Rockies. This book, however, will focus on the Algonquians of the eastern woodlands. These tribes were bonded by a similar language and a similar way of life.

# DAILY LIFE

The Algonquian-speaking Indians settled in northeastern America. These Indians made their homes in places now known as eastern New York, Long Island, New England, and areas around the Great Lakes. Some tribes established villages near the present-day Canadian cities of Quebec and Ottawa. Others pushed as far south as North Carolina. At the time of these settlements, the land was covered by thick forests. The Algonquians used the forest and every other natural resource the land and water had to offer to satisfy all their basic needs.

→

The Algonquians built small villages near rivers and lakes. Sometimes fewer than one hundred people lived in one village. Most of the Algonquians built dome-shaped homes called *wigwams*. Young trees, or saplings, were used to build the frame of the wigwam. The saplings were fashioned into poles with stone chisels and knives

[14]

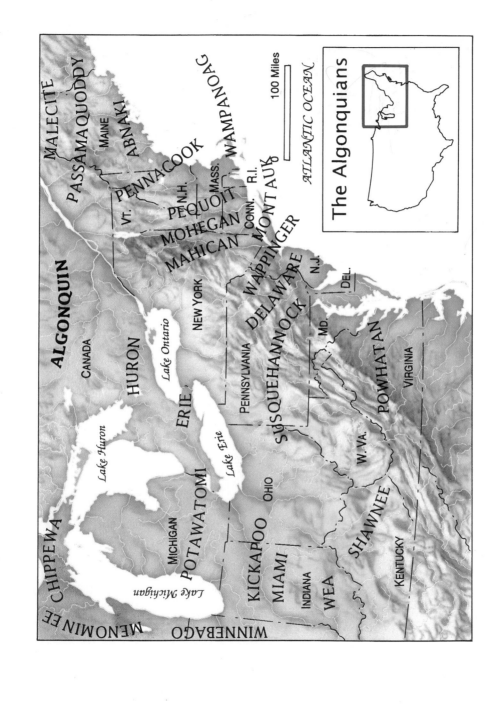

## The Algonquians

100 Miles

ATLANTIC OCEAN

MALECITE

PASSAMAQUODDY

ABNAKI

MAINE

PENNACOOK

WAMPANOAG

N.H.

Vt.

MASS.

PEQUOIT

R.I.

MONTAUK

MOHEGAN

CONN.

MAHICAN

WAPPINGER

DELAWARE

N.J.

SUSQUEHANNOCK

DEL.

NEW YORK

MD.

PENNSYLVANIA

POWHATAN

ALGONQUIN

CANADA

HURON

Lake Ontario

ERIE

Lake Erie

W.VA.

VIRGINIA

Lake Huron

POTAWATOMI

OHIO

SHAWNEE

MICHIGAN

KICKAPOO

MIAMI

INDIANA

WEA

KENTUCKY

Lake Michigan

CHIPPEWA

MENOMINEE

WINNEBAGO

made from beaver teeth. They were then placed into holes in the ground. This was usually done in a circular or a somewhat oval pattern. Poles opposite one another were bent at the top and tied together with roots or *sinew*. After the basic frame was constructed, more saplings were used to go around the structure and over the top of it. A small opening was left for a doorway. The wigwam frame was covered with mats the women wove from *cattail rushes*. When it was cold, large pieces of bark were used to cover the outside of the dwelling. Birchbark was used wherever birch trees grew. This bark was lightweight and could easily be rolled up and transported to another campsite.

In the center of the wigwam was a shallow pit used as a fireplace. Fires were built for heating the structure, for cooking, and for light. A hole in the middle of the roof was left open so the smoke could leave the wigwam. The hole could be covered with a slab of bark in case of high winds or heavy rains.

Platforms or shelves were also made from saplings. These were used as beds, seats, tables, and workplaces. Grass or reed mats covered the floor and walls. Mats, as well as animal skins, were used as bedding. Baskets, bowls, cooking utensils, and dried food were kept in the wigwam.

By today's standards, this dwelling was rather small. It was about 15 feet (4.57 m) wide. Usually one family

HERE YOU CAN SEE HOW
A WIGWAM WAS BUILT.

lived in it, which many times included one set of grand-parents. This wigwam was the most commonly built shelter among the Algonquians. However, some groups constructed homes that were cone-shaped (like a *teepee*). Though the shape was different, the construction and materials used were very similar.

Some villages included larger wigwams that were used as gathering places for ceremonies and rituals. As the years went by and fighting over village sites became more frequent, many Algonquian villages were sur-rounded by tall fences called *palisades*. These helped to protect them from enemy attacks.

➡

Just as nature helped provide shelter for the Algonqui-ans, nature also provided their clothing—nature, that is, along with the Indians' creativity. Animal skins and furs were the materials used in making clothing. Clothing was geared to the weather. Women wore long skirts of deerskin, and when it was cold, another skin was worn on the upper part of their bodies. Leggings up to the knee were worn when necessary.

Men wore nothing but a breechcloth during the warm months. A breechcloth was a thin piece of hide about 3 feet (.9 m) long. It was put between the legs and draped over a belt around the waist. There was a flap in the front and a flap in the back. Leggings were worn for protection as needed. When the weather got

AS ALGONQUIAN WOMEN WORKED AROUND
THE VILLAGE SITE, THEY WORE SIMPLE
DEERSKIN CLOTHING TO SHIELD THEM
FROM THE COLD.

colder, men usually wore a robe made of leather. Sometimes robes made from animal fur, such as bear or rabbit, were used.

Children wore no clothing at all when it was warm. To protect them from cold temperatures, robes were put over them. At ten years of age, they began to dress like adults.

Moccasins were worn by Algonquians of all ages. These were decorated with porcupine quills. Indians had much respect for the earth and making their footwear attractive was a way of showing their respect. Sometimes the children's moccasins had holes in the bottoms. Some Algonquians believed that evil spirits would not take the children if their shoes were in poor condition.

Both the Algonquian men and women mixed bear fat into their hair. This made it very shiny. Some added *soot* to the fat, making their hair extremely black. Most women wore their hair long. Some tied it back in a ponytail or braid, using leather strips or strings of *wampum*.

The men enjoyed wearing their hair in various styles. Some wore it long; some wore it braided. Others preferred to rid their heads of all hair except for a strip that went from the top of the head down to the back.

→

The Algonquian Indians fished, hunted, or farmed, depending on where they settled. Tribes who lived near

AN ALGONQUIAN WARRIOR'S OUTFIT

the coast and in the Great Lakes region depended upon fishing for their diets. Those who lived inland depended on the game they hunted, as well as the native plants they learned to grow.

Hooks, spears, and nets were used to catch fish. Hooks were made from small animal bones which were sharpened at each end. Sometimes the wishbones of birds were used as hooks. The Indians made spears from stone and nets from sinew. Off the coast of New England, salmon was plentiful. The tribes around the Great Lakes caught large amounts of pike and sturgeon.

For the tribes that hunted, bear, deer, and moose were among the large animals the men stalked. During hunting season, the families moved to a new campsite. They would stay there quite long—sometimes months at a time. Creativity was necessary during the hunt. Whenever possible, the hunters would steer their prey near water in hopes of driving the animal in. Capturing and killing were easier in water than on land since the animal could not move very fast in water.

Much of the hunting was done during the winter. When there was snow on the ground, the Indians could follow animal tracks more easily. The animals moved slower in the snow, giving the hunters an advantage. Many times the men would lure the animals to the edge of a cliff with a piece of meat as bait. Then they would

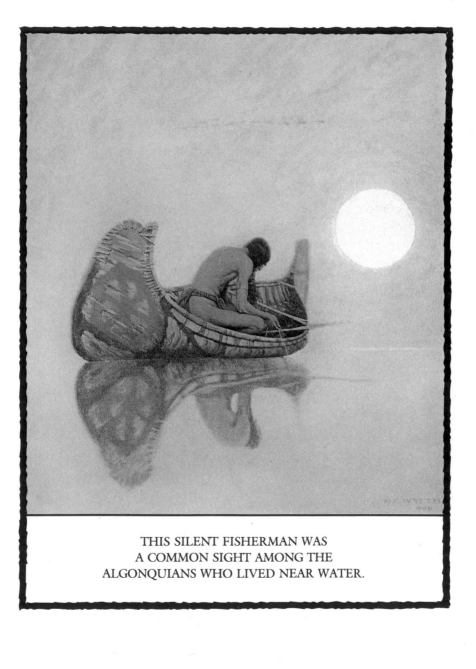

THIS SILENT FISHERMAN WAS
A COMMON SIGHT AMONG THE
ALGONQUIANS WHO LIVED NEAR WATER.

INDIANS USED SNOWSHOES TO MAKE
THEIR HUNT FOR BUFFALO A LITTLE
EASIER, AND HOPEFULLY SUCCESSFUL, TOO.

drive the surprised animals over the edge. Other men would be waiting below to zoom in for the kill.

Animals were hunted with bows and arrows. Bows were made from wood such as white oak, ash, or hickory. The bark was stripped from the wood and the wood cut to about 5 feet (1.5 m) long. It was then shaped, greased, and seasoned. Boys were taught to make bows when they were young—a skill used throughout their lives.

Deer sinew or tough plant fibers were used to string the bow. The string was twisted before each end was attached to the bow. Arrows were generally made from wood. The arrowheads were made from stone, bone, or shell. Anything sharp and strong could be used. The arrowheads were bound to the end of the arrow with sinew. Sometimes arrowheads were not needed. The ends of the wooden arrows could be sharpened and used alone when small animals were hunted. When birds were hunted, the end of the arrow would be rounded slightly as the impact of the arrow would be enough to kill the bird.

Large game were not the only animals the Indians hunted. Smaller game such as rabbit, porcupine, squirrel, mink, otter, and fowl were also sought. Smaller animals could be trapped. The Indians were very adept at making snares and traps in which to catch these animals.

A BOY IS TAUGHT HOW TO
FIX A BROKEN BOW.

Wild rice was the staple food of the Chippewa and Menominee Indians who lived around the Great Lakes. This grain grew in shallow fresh water and was harvested by the Indians. While the men poled a canoe through the marsh, the women would bend the stalks over the canoe and hit them with sticks. This caused the grain to fall to the bottom of the canoe.

Many Algonquian tribes discovered the sweet taste of maple sugar. *Sap* from maple trees was gathered in baskets in early spring. Syrup was made by boiling the sap. When boiled longer, syrup could be molded into a hard sugar substance. Maple sugar was used in most of the Indians' cooking.

Many Algonquians were expert farmers. The men had to take down large trees in order to make open garden space. First, a circle of wet clay was wrapped around the tree a few feet from the base. Then a fire was set at the bottom of the tree. The clay prevented the fire from spreading up the length of the trunk. After the base of the tree was weakened by the fire, the men used their stone axes to chop the tree down. The ashes from the burned wood were used as fertilizer for the garden.

Crops such as beans, corn, squash, pumpkins, sunflowers, and tobacco were grown. Originally these were plants that grew wild; the Algonquians, however, learned to *domesticate* them. Women and children did all the planting, harvesting, and preparation of food. Corn was

HARVESTING RICE REQUIRED
MORE THAN ONE PERSON.

planted in small hills. It is widely believed that a dead fish was buried in each hill to act as a fertilizer and make the corn grow stronger and larger. Beans and squash were planted between the hills of corn. As they grew, these vine plants climbed up the large cornstalks.

The Algonquians also gathered nuts, berries, and roots. Nuts and berries were used alone or in cakes. Beverages were also made from berries. The roots of some plants, such as sassafras, were used in making tea.

[28]

SMOKING A SUPPLY OF FISH ENABLED THE
ALGONQUIANS TO STORE IT FOR THE WINTER,
WHEN FRESH FOOD WOULD BE SCARCE.

Meat and fish were cooked over a fire in pots made of bark, wood, or clay. Sometimes the meat was boiled using red-hot stones, which were put in the water. Other times it was cooked on sticks. Wild onion and garlic helped to flavor the meats and vegetables. To preserve the meats, the Indians dried or smoked it. Crops and berries were also dried and stored for the winter. Getting ready for the long cold months was a big job.

# RELIGION

The Algonquians believed in one powerful supreme spirit. Some tribes called this spirit "Manitou." Manitou controlled all things in everyday life. This supreme spirit helped the Indians with growing crops and hunting for food. Besides Manitou, the Algonquians also believed in many other spirits—good as well as evil. The evil spirit was responsible for anything bad that happened. All things in nature were thought to be alive with the Manitou spirit. Trees, animals, fish, as well as lakes, rivers, rocks, the sun, moon, wind, and rain, were all believed to have supernatural powers.

A man or woman who the Algonquians thought was in contact with the world of spirits was called a *shaman*. A shaman received his supernatural powers from dreams or visions. Often a shaman was called upon to make contact with the spirit world at hunting or planting season. The Indians thought this would ensure a plentiful food supply. Shamans also knew about curing illnesses. They used certain herbs as medicine and were knowledgeable about setting broken bones. Shamans were respected as well as feared.

Some of the tribes around the Great Lakes region, including the Chippewa and the Winnebago, formed a society called the Midewiwin Society, or Grand Medicine Society. This was a secret group formed to cure illness. They used special objects, sang special songs, and had special rituals to get in contact with the spirit world.

A SHAMAN MIXES MEDICINE
IN HIS WIGWAM.

Besides shamans, the Algonquians also had priests. The priests led prayer services for large groups, unlike shamans, who were usually called upon by single families. The Algonquians called their priests *powwows*. To become a priest, one had to have extensive training. The priests had gathering places for rituals and ceremonies. *Powwow* is an Algonquian word that today means "a get-together" or "a meeting."

Ceremonies were held at different times of the year.

CEREMONIES AND FEASTS BROKE
THE ROUTINE OF DAY-TO-DAY LIVING.
HERE, THE SNOW-SHOE DANCE OF THE
OJIBWAS (WHO LIVED IN THE GREAT
LAKES REGION) IS PORTRAYED.

THIS EXHIBIT AT THE AMERICAN MUSEUM
OF NATURAL HISTORY SHOWS A THUNDER
PIPE CEREMONY. NOTE THE ELABORATE
PIPE AND OTHER OBJECTS INVOLVED
IN THE CEREMONY.

Planting season, harvest time, and hunting season were all times to ask Manitou, or the "Great Spirit" as white settlers would later call it, to look after them. Music and dancing were part of the ceremonies. Drums, rattles, whistles, flutes, and singing all added to the excitement. A form of tobacco was used at all of these occasions. The Indians believed the smoke had the power to take their messages up to the spirit world.

# ARTS AND CRAFTS

Everything the Algonquians made served a purpose. At times, however, the Indians would decorate the items to make them more attractive. Porcupine quills and bird feathers were used to trim clothing, moccasins, pouches, and sometimes baskets. Most often the men killed the porcupines, but at times women and children found quills scattered throughout the woods. After being flattened and moistened, the quills could be woven into material. Sometimes white quills were dyed. Berries, flower petals, and wild grapes were used for red, yellow, and black dye. Quillwork was hard and slow. Today very little quillwork is done.

Another material used for decoration was moose hair. Hair taken from the mane and *jowls* of the moose was washed and dyed. It was used as thread. With this hair, women embroidered designs on moccasins and hides.

FEATHERS MAKE THIS HEADDRESS
DRAMATIC—WITHOUT THEM, IT WOULD
SIMPLY BE A HEADBAND.

Birch bark was highly prized by those Algonquians living in the Northeast and the Great Lakes region. Birch bark is waterproof, and thus does not rot easily. To make a birch-bark canoe, Algonquians had to fell a few trees. This was usually done in the spring because the bark was strongest after the winter. It was also moist and easier to work with. Other trees such as arborvitae and white cedar were used to make the floor and ribs of the canoe. The women used roots from plants to sew the pieces of bark together. Gum from trees was thickened by boiling and then used to seal the seams of the bark. Most birch-bark canoes were about 18 feet (5.48 m) in length. One man could carry a canoe of this size. The largest canoes were about 40 feet (12 m) long. It only took two men to carry one this big. Because of all the streams, rivers, and lakes in the Northeast, birch-bark canoes were an important method of transportation for the Algonquians.

Baskets of all sizes and shapes were also made from birch bark. Some had lids, others did not. One type of storage basket with a very tight-fitting lid was called a *wigwâmot*. The Algonquian women would often make designs on the bark. By scraping the light outer bark, a dark layer was revealed underneath. Birch-bark baskets are still made by some Algonquians today. Stencils help them to create lovely patterns on the bark.

BUILDING A BIRCH-BARK CANOE WAS A
COMPLICATED PROJECT, BUT ONE THAT WAS
NECESSARY IN ORDER FOR THE ALGONQUIANS
TO TRAVEL THE WATERWAYS IN THEIR AREA.

But birch bark was not the only material used to make baskets. Corn husks, grasses, and reeds, as well as other types of bark, were also used. Baskets were important for carrying, gathering, and storing food. The tightness of the weave depended on what the basket would be used for.

*Cradleboards* were yet another item made from available birch bark. Again, this was the preferred material because of its light weight. Babies were put into cradleboards and then carried around on their mothers' backs. The youngster was tucked into animal hide that was attached to the cradleboard. Sometimes a wooden shelf was built at the bottom to support the child's feet. At the top, a wooden awning protected the baby from too much sun, as well as from pesty insects. The back of the cradleboard was sometimes decorated with attractive patterns scraped or burned into the bark. When the mother was busy gardening, she would hang the cradleboard (baby and all) from the limb of a tree. Until they

THIS RATTLE WAS MADE FROM BARK.

A SQUAW CAN BRING HER CHILD WHEREVER
SHE GOES BY CARRYING THE BABY IN A
CRADLEBOARD ON HER BACK.

could walk, Algonquian babies were kept in cradle-boards most of the day. Some of the more traditional Algonquian tribes still use them today.

Rolled-up birch bark was used to make a *mozigidâgan*. This is the Algonquian word for moose call. It was shaped like a *megaphone*. The men would make noises into the mozigidâgan that attracted moose during mating season.

Some Algonquians made very warm and soft blankets out of rabbit fur. It took hundreds of rabbits to make one large blanket. The fur was woven rather loosely, making a beautiful, warm "thermal" blanket.

Those tribes living near the coast gathered shells, from which they made beautiful beads called wampum. The shells used were a hard and thick clamshell called *quahog*. Sharp stones helped the Indians get to the inside of the shell. It was very hard work and took a lot of time. Small beads were fashioned from pieces of the shell. They were purple or white in color.

With very primitive tools, a hole was drilled through the middle of each bead. Then the wampum was strung on threadlike material. Wampum made lovely belts, necklaces, and bracelets. Today most people think of wampum as Indian money, but this was not the original purpose for making wampum. The Algonquians, like all other Indian tribes in the United States, had no written language. Wampum belts were a means of communica-

WAMPUM BELTS WERE A WAY OF
COMMUNICATING AND TELLING HISTORY.
THE TOP BELT WAS GIVEN TO THE CHIPPEWA
BY THE DELAWARE INDIANS.

tion among the different tribes. Designs sewn into the belts had various meanings. Wampum belts recorded information, declared treaties or wars, and were used to send messages to neighboring tribes. After the Europeans came to North America, the Algonquians often used wampum as money or for trading goods. The purple beads were worth twice as much as the white beads.

# GAMES

The Algonquians enjoyed playing games of all sorts. Men played with men and women played with women, and children were left to amuse themselves with their running and jumping contests. Often, the children imitated adult games.

Guessing games were very popular—and so was gambling on the outcome of such games. One guessing game involved four moccasins and four objects. (Four was a popular number because of the four directions: north, south, east, and west.) One of the objects was marked. Each team tried to guess under which moccasin the opposing team hid the marked object. Usually a big crowd gathered for guessing games. Music was played and many bets were placed. Sometimes the games were played until a man had lost everything he owned.

*Tobogganing* in winter was a fun pastime for all. Another winter game was called snowsnake. In this, a long stick was thrown down a snow-covered hill.

GAMES ADDED FUN TO LIFE AND FOSTERED
A SENSE OF COMPETITIVENESS. THESE
ALGONQUIANS ARE PLAYING A BALL GAME
THAT LOOKS VERY MUCH LIKE FIELD HOCKEY.

Whoever threw the stick the farthest won the game. Bets were also placed on the outcome of this game.

Other games involved tests of skill. *Lacrosse* was enjoyed by some Algonquian tribes such as the Menominee, Passamaquoddy, and Winnebago. Running games and pretend battles were played very competitively. Survival lessons were taught through the games.

# SOCIAL AND POLITICAL LIFE

The family was the basic social unit for the Algonquians. This of course included the father, mother, and children. It also included people related to either the father's family or the mother's family. Some tribes were *patrilineal,* meaning the children were members of their father's family. Some tribes were *matrilineal,* meaning the children were members of their mother's family. Children could not belong to both families. *Anthropologists* call this the clan system. In a patrilineal society, the father and his children belonged to the same clan. The mother, even though she lived and worked with her immediate family, was considered a member of a different clan.

In every clan, the young people learned about the past from the old people. Since there was no written language, stories were passed down *orally*. There were many legends about how different tribes came to be.

KISH-KE-KOSH, A FOX BRAVE,
APPEARS READY FOR BATTLE.

Most Indians believed they descended from certain animals. Because of this, animals were highly respected. For example, after eating fish, an Algonquian Indian always threw the bones back into the water so the fish spirit could return home.

→

There were well over fifty Algonquian tribes. These tribes were broken down into smaller groups called *bands*. Bands were made up of several *extended families* who lived together in villages. Each village had a chief, called a *sachem*. Once or twice a year the tribal members would get together for a meeting.

Because the Algonquians were basically hunters, the bands often moved in search of food. Sometimes fights over hunting grounds, village sites, general misunderstandings, and revenge took place among the various Algonquian bands and tribes. Their "wars" were really quick raids involving small groups of men armed with bows and arrows and *tomahawks*. For the most part, however, the Algonquians were a peaceful group with little political organization, with the exception of the Abenakis of Maine and the Powhattans of Virginia, who were both more politically established.

# MEETING THE EUROPEANS

Imagine the surprise the coastal Algonquians felt when they saw enormous ships on the water. What did the Indians think as they watched strangely clad men unload unusual items?

At first the Indians and the Europeans were friendly toward one another. The Algonquians were fascinated by the guns, metal tools, cloth, beads, and other things brought from Europe. And the Europeans needed help from the Indians. They needed to learn how to survive in this strange new world. An Algonquian Indian named Massasoit, chief of the Wampanoag tribe, gave the settlers the help they so badly needed. He and one of his men, named Squanto, taught the Pilgrims how to plant crops, hunt game, and build shelters. The Europeans were introduced to new foods such as baked beans, *hominy,* and *succotash.* After the harvest of 1621, the Pilgrims invited Massasoit and his tribe to a huge feast. Although such celebrations were common among the

THE PILGRIMS RECEIVED MASSASOIT WITH
GREAT FANFARE. AFTER ALL, MASSASOIT
HELPED THE SETTLERS TO SURVIVE BY
TEACHING THEM SKILLS THEY NEEDED
IN THEIR NEW HOMELAND.

Indians long before the coming of the Europeans, this was the beginning of our traditional Thanksgiving celebration.

The arrival of the Europeans brought changes to both the Indians and the white people's way of life. Native cultures were shared. Trading took place. Many Indians began to kill animals just for their fur, as the European demand for fur grew. In return, the Algonquians received luxurious European items they had never before known—items which were not available from nature.

Some of the French Jesuits who settled in the new world were Catholic missionaries. They taught their religion to the Algonquians. Some Indians converted to this religion, while others kept to their old beliefs.

A few Algonquian tribes formed confederacies, hoping to become stronger and more united. One such group was the Wappinger Confederacy. They lived in the area today known as Manhattan, Westchester, and the Bronx in New York State. It was one of the Wappinger groups who, in 1626, supposedly sold Manhattan Island to the Dutch for $24.00 worth of goods. That island today is the center of New York City.

Soon after the Europeans began settling in the new world, they became greedy for land. Battles broke out between the new settlers and the Indians. Land, to the Algonquians, was a gift from Manitou for all to use.

GEORGE WASHINGTON
PRESIDENT 1793.

THIS GEORGE WASHINGTON PEACE MEDAL
WAS GIVEN TO A GROUP OF INDIANS ALONG WITH
A TREATY IN 1793. UNFORTUNATELY, THE
WHITE SETTLERS BROKE ALMOST EVERY TREATY
THEY EVER SIGNED WITH NATIVE AMERICANS.

They did not understand what buying and selling meant. When treaties were signed, the Indians thought they gave the white people the right to use the land. They did not know it meant they could no longer use the land themselves. When the white settlers forced the Indians off the land, more bloody battles took place. Many lives were lost on both sides. Unfortunately for the Algonquians, their bows and arrows were no match for the sleek guns of the Europeans.

When the Europeans arrived in the new world, they also brought disease. Outbreaks of smallpox and measles were common. The Algonquians had no resistance to these diseases, and some Algonquian tribes were completely wiped out by these illnesses.

Liquor was another item introduced to the Indians by the Europeans. This was something the Indians had no experience with and it proved to be a downfall for them. Some settlers would give the Indians liquor and then take advantage of their *intoxication*.

More and more Europeans came to North America. Soon there were more whites than Indians, and the natives were pushed westward in the settlers' quest for more land. The Algonquian population was drastically reduced as disease and years of war took their toll.

# THE ALGONQUIANS TODAY

The modern world has much to thank the Indians for. Among the things they introduced to the Europeans were corn, potatoes, turkey, beans, squash, and maple syrup. Medicines such as *witch hazel, ipecac, quinine,* and oil of wintergreen were first used by the Indians. Moccasins, snowshoes, toboggans, and *hammocks* were all items the Indians devised. U.S. highways have been built on Indian trails. Indian words are common in daily life. About half of the states in the United States, as well as many lakes, rivers, mountains, towns, and counties, are named from Indian words.

Today many Algonquians live on *reservations* in the eastern United States and Canada. A reservation is land provided by the government for Indian use. Some reservations have schools, day care centers, medical facilities, tourist attractions, and businesses located on the premises. These provide employment for some of the people. Other reservations are not as fortunate.

SOME RESERVATION SCHOOLS TEACH TRIBAL
HISTORY AND LANGUAGE IN ADDITION
TO BASICS SUCH AS ENGLISH AND MATH.

AS IS TRUE IN MANY SCHOOLS NOW, COMPUTERS
HELP RESERVATION STUDENTS TO UNDERSTAND
CONCEPTS AND PRACTICE NEW SKILLS.

While many Algonquians have adopted a more modern life-style, there are those who choose to practice and preserve the old traditions. Some of these people live on the Rapid Lake Reserve located near Quebec, Canada. Between 200 and 400 Algonquin Indians (the tribe from which the name Algonquian is derived) live there. They hunt in the *nopimâk,* or bush, which is the wooded area surrounding their log cabins. Though these Indians are mostly traditional, some modern-day conveniences aid them. For example, snowmobiles and guns are now used when they hunt.

Some of these Indians make a living as hunting guides, firefighters, or lumberjacks. Others choose to leave the reservation for months at a time to work on mink farms in Ontario and Wayne counties in western New York.

There are approximately 300 Delaware Indians living as farmers in Oklahoma. The largest group of Algonquians in the United States and Canada is the Chippewa. Their population is about 250,000. Some of these people live in towns or cities; others live on reservations.

But life on reservations is hard. Sadly, alcoholism is common and unemployment is high. The Algonquians, however, are a proud people. Many are trying to preserve their heritage in modern America. They should be saluted for what their ancestors have contributed to this "new world," their native land.

# GLOSSARY

**anthropologist**   one who studies humans and their societies

**archeologist**   one who studies the history and culture of people who lived in the past by discovering and studying the things they left behind

**bands**   groups of several extended families living together in a village

**cattail rushes**   tall marsh plants with long flat leaves

**cradleboard**   an item made from wood and animal hide, and used to hold a baby

**domesticate**   to tame; to train for household use

**extended family**   family group that includes grandparents, aunts, uncles, and cousins, in addition to the immediate family of parents and children

**hammock**   a swinging bed or couch

*hominy*   an Algonquian food made from corn, which is boiled or fried

*intoxication*   a state of being drunk from consuming alcohol

*ipecac*   a tropical plant used to make medicine

*jowls*   soft and relaxed skin near the lower jaw and throat

*lacrosse*   a sport in which players use a long-handled basket to catch and throw a ball into an opposing team's goal

*matrilineal*   tracing descent through the mother's side

*megaphone*   a cone-shaped device used to magnify sounds

*orally*   by way of mouth; spoken

*palisade*   tall fence

*patrilineal*   tracing descent through the father's side

*powwow*   Indian priest; a get-together or meeting

*quahog*   thick clam shell

*quinine*   substance made from cinchona bark used in medicine

*reservation*   land provided by the government for Indian use *sachem*   Indian chief

*sap*   a sticky liquid that comes from maple trees, which is used to make syrup or maple sugar

*shaman*   an Indian healer said to be in contact with the spirit world

*sinew*   tendon

*soot*   a black powdery substance that is left over after something is burned

*Stone Age*   a prehistoric time during which humans used tools made of stone

*succotash*   an Algonquian food made by cooking together lima beans and corn

*teepee*   a cone-shaped dwelling made from saplings covered with animal skins

*toboggan*   long, flat-bottomed sled made of thin wood curving up at one end

*tomahawk*   an ax-like weapon

*wampum*   beads made from quahog

*wigwam*   dome-shaped dwelling

*witch hazel*   soothing lotion made from plants of the witch hazel family

# FOR FURTHER READING

Baity, Elizabeth Chesley. *Americans Before Columbus*. New York: The Viking Press, 1961.

Baldwin, Gordon C. *How Indians Really Lived*. New York: G. P. Putnam's Sons, 1967.

Bjorkland, Karna L. *The Indians of Northeastern America*. New York: Dodd, Mead & Co., 1969.

Grant, Bruce. *American Indians Yesterday and Today*. New York: E. P. Dutton & Co., Inc., 1960.

Johnston, Johanna. *The Indians and the Strangers*. New York: Dodd, Mead & Co., 1972.

Stan, Susan. *The Ojibwe*. Vero Beach, Fla.: Rourke Publications, Inc., 1989.

Wolfson, Evelyn. *From Abenaki to Zuni: A Dictionary of Native American Tribes*. New York: Walker and Company, 1988.

# INDEX

*Patricia Ryon Quiri* lives in Palm Harbor, Florida, with her husband and three sons. She is a former elementary school teacher and has an elementary education degree from Alfred University in New York State. Ms. Quiri is an active parent volunteer in the Pinellas County School System. Other Franklin Watts books written by Ms. Quiri include *Dating, Alexander Graham Bell,* and *Metamorphosis.*